Bruce Smith

GREATEST DEFENSIVE LINEMEN

Michael Strahan

NFL HALL OF FAMERS

GREATEST DEFENSIVE LINEMEN

JOE TISCHLER

CREATIVE SPORTS

Joe Greene

CREATIVE EDUCATION / CREATIVE PAPERBACKS

Published by Creative Education and Creative Paperbacks
P.O. Box 227, Mankato, Minnesota 56002
Creative Education and Creative Paperbacks
are imprints of The Creative Company
www.thecreativecompany.us

Design and production by Blue Design (www.bluedes.com)
Art direction by Rita Marshall

Images by Getty Images/Al Bello, 28, Al Messerschmidt, 29, Allen Dean Steele, cover, Bill Eppridge/Time Life Pictures, 7, Brian Killian, 2, David Madison, 25, Ezra Shaw, 30, Focus On Sport, 6, 7, 12, 15, 18, 21, George Gojkovich, 9, Gregory Shamus, 7, Jonathan Daniel, 26, Kidwiler Collection, 7, Michael Zagaris, 6, NFL, 4–5, 11, 32, NFL/Pro Football Hall Of Fame, 6, Richard Stagg, 17, Rick Stewart, 1, Robert Riger, 3, 14, Stephen Dunn, 22, TIMOTHY A. CLARY, 6, Vic Milton, 19; Wikimedia Commons/Gonzo fan2007, cover (background), public domain, 10

Library of Congress Cataloging-in-Publication Data
Names: Tischler, Joe, author.
Title: Greatest defensive linemen / Joe Tischler.
Description: Mankato, Minnesota : Creative Education and Creative Paperbacks, 2026. | Series: Creative sports. NFL Hall of Famers | Includes index. | Audience: Ages 8–12 | Audience: Grades 4–6 | Summary: "Photo-driven and stat-filled, this middle-grade NFL title showcases 11 of pro football's greatest defensive linemen enshrined in the Hall of Fame, from Deacon Jones and Alan Page to Reggie White and Michael Strahan"—Provided by publisher.
Identifiers: LCCN 2024048113 (print) | LCCN 2024048114 (ebook) | ISBN 9798889896135 (library binding) | ISBN 9781682777794 (paperback) | ISBN 9798889896937 (ebook)
Subjects: LCSH: Football players—United States—Biography—Juvenile literature. | Football—Defense—Juvenile literature. | Pro Football Hall of Fame (U.S.)—Juvenile literature.
Classification: LCC GV939.A1 T54 2026 (print) | LCC GV939.A1 (ebook) | DDC 796.332092/2 [B]—dc23/eng/20241202
LC record available at https://lccn.loc.gov/2024048113
LC ebook record available at https://lccn.loc.gov/2024048114

Printed in India

Deacon Jones

60

MOSS
81

TAYLOR
56

42

CONTENTS

Introduction 8

Deacon Jones 10

Bob Lilly 12

Joe Greene 14

Alan Page 16

Randy White 18

Jack Youngblood 20

Reggie White 22

Bruce Smith 24

John Randle 26

Warren Sapp 28

Michael Strahan 30

Index 32

TIMEOUT

Defensive Lineman Duties 11

Grin and Bear It 21

Position Changes 29

INTRODUCTION

It's third down and long. Time to shut down the offense. Defensive end Reggie White is primed and ready. His target? The quarterback. He does a club move around the offensive lineman and brings the quarterback down. Job done!

One of the main jobs of a defensive lineman is to tackle, or sack, the quarterback. Doing so gives the defense a charge. It also puts the offense in a hole. The defensive line is made up of defensive ends and defensive tackles. They're some of the biggest, most fearsome players. All defensive linemen who play for the National Football League (NFL) are at the top of their game. But only a handful can be called Hall of Famers.

The Pro Football Hall of Fame honors 378 past players, coaches, and sport contributors. Of those, about 40 are defensive linemen. This book highlights 11 Hall of Fame defensive linemen whose careers reached above and beyond. This list isn't a ranking. Players are ordered by the year they were enshrined.

Reggie White

DEACON JONES (1938–2013)
DEFENSIVE END
LOS ANGELES RAMS SEASONS: 1961–71; SAN DIEGO CHARGERS SEASONS: 1972–73; WASHINGTON REDSKINS SEASON: 1974
HALL OF FAME CLASS: 1980
AWARDS/HONORS: MEMBER OF NFL 75TH/100TH ANNIVERSARY TEAMS, 8X PRO BOWL, 8X ALL-PRO (5X FIRST TEAM), 1960S NFL ALL-DECADE TEAM, 2X NFL DEFENSIVE PLAYER OF THE YEAR

DEACON JONES

David "Deacon" Jones was one of the greatest defensive linemen of all time. People credit him with coining the term "sack." Even so, Jones played at a time when sacks were not counted as official statistics. That didn't happen until 1982. Researchers went back through gamebooks and counted sack totals from 1960 to 1981. Jones would have led the NFL in sacks five times, including two 22-sack seasons in 1964 and 1968. The official single-season record is 22.5. Jones would have had 173.5 career sacks—good for third most all-time.

With the Rams, Jones was a member of the "Fearsome Foursome" defensive line. It featured Jones and fellow future Hall of Famer Merlin Olsen. Jones earned First Team All-Pro honors five straight seasons. He played in seven straight Pro Bowls. Twice, the Newspaper Enterprise Association named him NFL Defensive Player of the Year. Jones was traded late in his career to the San Diego Chargers. He earned his eighth Pro Bowl selection in his first year in San Diego.

After his playing career, Jones acted. He appeared in several television shows and films. He also became involved in community efforts. He founded the Deacon Jones Foundation. It helps young people and the communities in which they live.

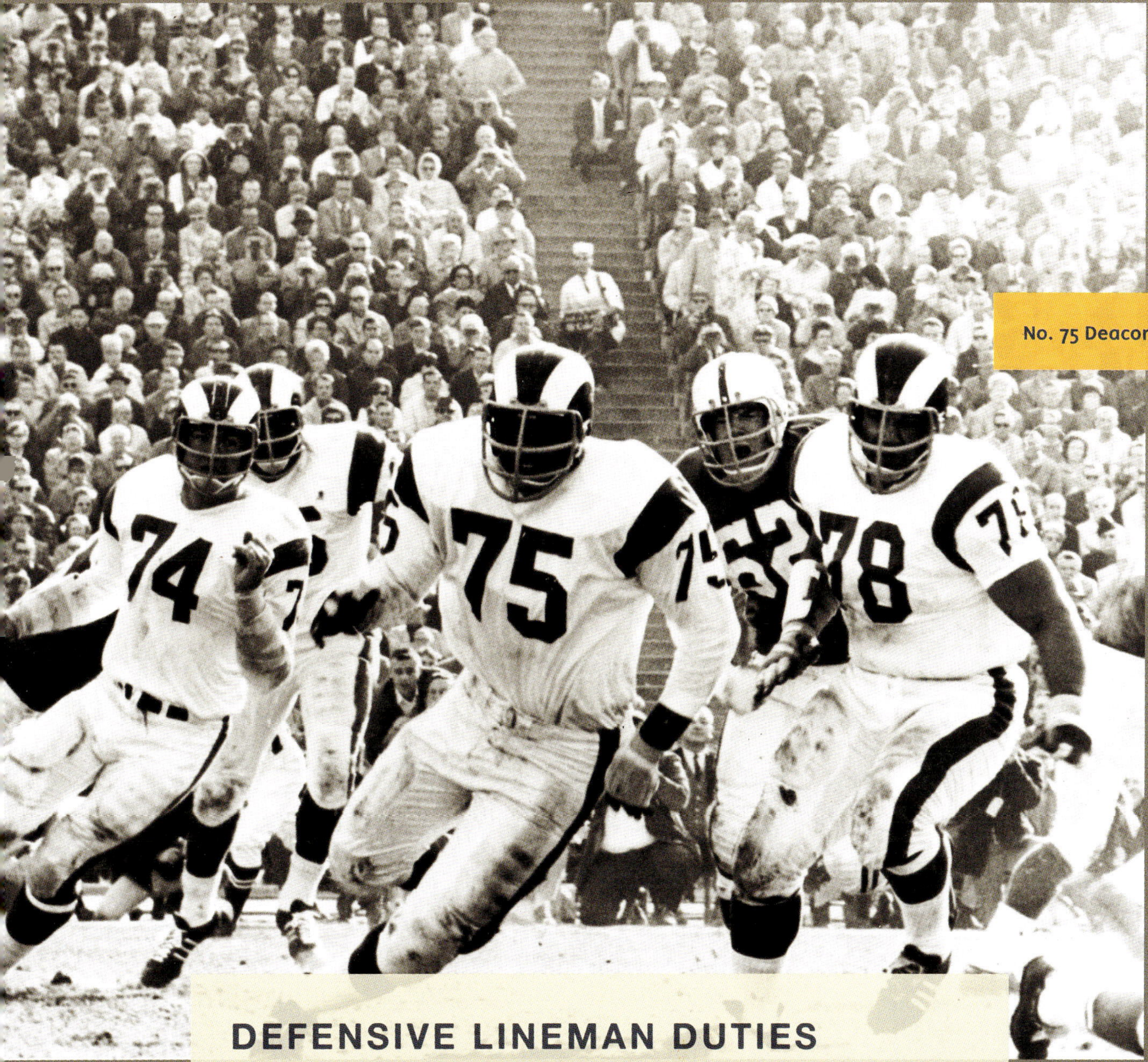

No. 75 Deacon Jones

DEFENSIVE LINEMAN DUTIES

The defensive line is the first line of defense. Linebackers are behind them. And the defensive backs act as the last line. Defensive linemen rush the quarterback. They either tackle him or cause him to do something he's not ready for. They also clog up any lanes that the other team's running back might use. Defensive tackles line up toward the middle of the line. Defensive ends line up toward the outside. These two positions can also be called nose tackles and edge rushers. Defensive linemen are typically the biggest players (in terms of weight) on defense.

BOB LILLY

BOB LILLY (1939–)
DEFENSIVE END
DALLAS COWBOYS SEASONS: 1961–74
HALL OF FAME CLASS: 1980
AWARDS/HONORS: MEMBER OF NFL 75TH/100TH ANNIVERSARY TEAMS, 11X PRO BOWL, 9X ALL-PRO (7X FIRST TEAM), 1960S/1970S NFL ALL-DECADE TEAMS, SUPER BOWL CHAMPION

Nicknamed "Mr. Cowboy," Bob Lilly was the first-ever draft choice of the Dallas Cowboys. They selected him in the first round of the 1961 NFL Draft. He played all levels of football in the state of Texas, including at Texas Christian University. Lilly was the first career player with the Cowboys to be honored in the Pro Football Hall of Fame. Lilly spent his first two years with the Cowboys at defensive end. He then moved to defensive tackle in his third season.

Lilly's best season may have been 1971. He was runner-up in the voting for NFL Defensive Player of the Year. He was also named First Team All-Pro for the seventh time. Most importantly, he helped the Cowboys win their first Super Bowl championship. It was a 24–3 win over the Miami Dolphins. Lilly was responsible for one of the most memorable plays. His 29-yard sack of Dolphins quarterback Bob Griese is still the longest sack in Super Bowl history. Lilly played in 11 Pro Bowls. He was also a member of two NFL All-Decade Teams.

Lilly had a stellar 14-year career, despite being routinely double- and triple-teamed. He said this about finding a way to make the play: "You have to be able to spin out of a block, recognize a play immediately, and then react accordingly. I figure I'm as strong as anyone else; so getting the job done becomes a matter of pride and determination."

JOE GREENE

JOE GREENE (1946–)
DEFENSIVE END
PITTSBURGH STEELERS SEASONS: 1969–81
HALL OF FAME CLASS: 1987
AWARDS/HONORS: MEMBER OF NFL 75TH/100TH ANNIVERSARY TEAMS, 10X PRO BOWL, 8X ALL-PRO (5X FIRST TEAM), 2X NFL DEFENSIVE PLAYER OF THE YEAR, 1970S NFL ALL-DECADE TEAMS, NFL MAN OF THE YEAR, 4X SUPER BOWL CHAMPION

One of the greatest defensive tackles of all time was "Mean" Joe Greene. He made life miserable for opposing teams. Greene came out of North Texas State University. He was selected in the first round of the 1969 NFL Draft by the Pittsburgh Steelers. The Steelers were a terrible team

Greene's first season. But it was not because of him. Pittsburgh won just one game in 1969. Greene, however, was named NFL Defensive Rookie of the Year. He made his first of 10 Pro Bowl appearances, too. He became the best player on the famed "Steel Curtain" defense of the 1970s. By the time he retired in 1981, Greene and the Steelers were four-time Super Bowl champions.

Contrary to his nickname, Greene was a nice guy. In 1979, he was named NFL Man of the Year for his work in the community. He also appeared in one of the most memorable Super Bowl commercials for Coca-Cola. In it, he rebuffed his "mean" guy attitude. "I just want people to remember me as being a good player and not really mean," Greene said. "I want to be remembered for playing 13 years and contributing to 4 championship teams. I would like to be remembered for maybe setting a standard for others to achieve."

Greene earned two NFL Defensive Player of the Year honors. One came in 1972. The other was in 1974. That year, the Steelers won the first of their four Super Bowl championships in a six-year span.

ALAN PAGE

ALAN PAGE (1945–)
DEFENSIVE TACKLE
MINNESOTA VIKINGS SEASONS: 1967–78; CHICAGO BEARS SEASONS: 1978–81
HALL OF FAME CLASS: 1988
AWARDS/HONORS: MEMBER OF NFL 100TH ANNIVERSARY TEAM, 9X PRO BOWL, 8X ALL-PRO (5X FIRST TEAM), 2X NFL DEFENSIVE PLAYER OF THE YEAR, NFL MOST VALUABLE PLAYER, 1970S NFL ALL-DECADE TEAM

Alan Page was born and raised in Canton, Ohio. He graduated from Canton Central Catholic High School in 1963. That was the same year the Pro Football Hall of Fame opened. In fact, Page worked on a construction team that helped build it! Years later, he would be honored inside its walls.

In 1971, while playing for the Minnesota Vikings, Page became the first defensive player to be named NFL Most Valuable Player. He was part of the famed "Purple People Eaters" defensive line. It was called that because of the purple jerseys the players wore. It was also in reference to a popular song from the 1950s. Page helped lead the Vikings to four Super Bowl appearances. But the team fell short every time. Page is one of only 11 Vikings to have played for the squad in all four Super Bowls.

Page was named NFL Defensive Player of the Year in 1971 and 1973. He was voted to nine straight Pro Bowls, too. He earned All-Pro honors eight straight seasons, including five First Team honors. Unofficially, Page recorded 148.5 sacks over his 15-year career. His career high of 18 sacks came in 1976, the last of the Vikings four Super Bowl appearances.

While playing for the Vikings, Page attended law school. He was later elected to the Minnesota Supreme Court. He was the first African American to serve on that court. In 2018, Page was awarded the Presidential Medal of Freedom.

No. 54 Randy White

RANDY WHITE (1953–)
DEFENSIVE TACKLE
DALLAS COWBOYS SEASONS: 1975–88
HALL OF FAME CLASS: 1994
AWARDS/HONORS: MEMBER OF NFL 100TH ANNIVERSARY TEAM, 9X PRO BOWL, 8X ALL-PRO (7X FIRST TEAM), 1980S NFL ALL-DECADE TEAM, SUPER BOWL CHAMPION, SUPER BOWL CO-MVP

RANDY WHITE

Only 10 defensive players in NFL history have been named Most Valuable Player (MVP) of the Super Bowl. Randy White was one of them. He earned it while playing defensive tackle for the Dallas Cowboys against the Denver Broncos in Super Bowl XII (12). He shared co-MVP honors with Harvey Martin. White was part of the defense that forced eight Denver turnovers. The Cowboys beat the Broncos 27–10.

White was the second overall selection of the 1975 NFL Draft by the Dallas Cowboys. He played defensive end his first year and linebacker his second. He switched to defensive tackle in year three (1977), and his career took off. He earned the first of his nine straight Pro Bowl appearances and led the Cowboys to the Super Bowl championship. He unofficially recorded 16 sacks in 1978. That season, he was named First Team All-Pro for the first time. He received that honor in six of the next seven seasons. In NFL Defensive Player of the Year voting from 1980 to 1984, White was all the buzz. His name was in the top five every year, including two runner-up instances.

White's nickname was "the Manster"—half man, half monster. Reflecting on the qualities needed to play pro football, White said, "Strength is important. You need a combination of strength, speed, and mobility or agility. I know I have good strength, but without the speed and agility to go with it, I would not be playing major league football."

JACK YOUNGBLOOD

JACK YOUNGBLOOD (1950–)
DEFENSIVE END
LOS ANGELES RAMS SEASONS: 1971–84
HALL OF FAME CLASS: 2001
AWARDS/HONORS: 7X PRO BOWL, 8X ALL-PRO (5X FIRST TEAM), 1970S NFL ALL-DECADE TEAM

The Los Angeles Rams drafted Jack Youngblood in the first round of the 1971 NFL Draft. He started his career playing behind future Hall of Famer David "Deacon" Jones at defensive end. The Rams thought so much of Youngblood's talent that they traded Jones before the 1972 season. That led to 14 years with the club. Youngblood set a Rams record of 201 consecutive games played. He missed only one, in his final season. Youngblood unofficially led the NFL in sacks in 1974 with 15 and in 1979 with 18. In 1974, he earned his first of five First Team All-Pro honors. He unofficially recorded 151.5 sacks over his career.

The Rams were a force during Youngblood's long career. Los Angeles made the playoffs 10 times and reached the Super Bowl once following the 1979 season. Youngblood's best game may have been a 1975 NFC Divisional Playoff game against the St. Louis Cardinals. In it, he returned an interception 47 yards for a touchdown. He also recorded one sack, forced a fumble, and blocked an extra-point attempt. The Rams won, 35–23.

Youngblood went into acting and broadcasting following his playing career. He got involved in a number of charities, too. He opened the Jack Youngblood Center for NeuroEnhancement in Florida. The facility treats symptoms of traumatic brain injury. Youngblood also helps former NFL players in need through the Gridiron Greats Assistance Fund.

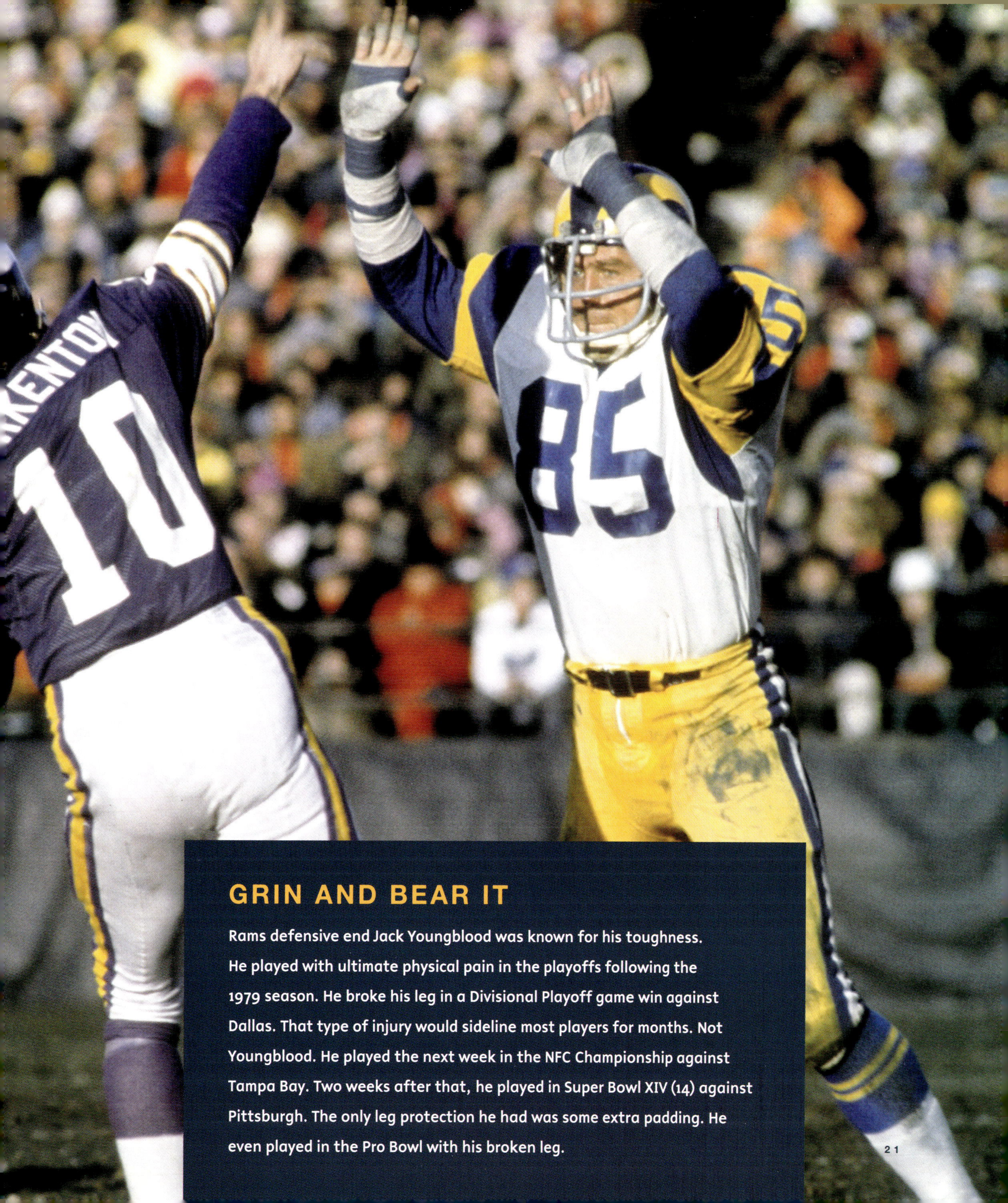

GRIN AND BEAR IT

Rams defensive end Jack Youngblood was known for his toughness. He played with ultimate physical pain in the playoffs following the 1979 season. He broke his leg in a Divisional Playoff game win against Dallas. That type of injury would sideline most players for months. Not Youngblood. He played the next week in the NFC Championship against Tampa Bay. Two weeks after that, he played in Super Bowl XIV (14) against Pittsburgh. The only leg protection he had was some extra padding. He even played in the Pro Bowl with his broken leg.

REGGIE WHITE

REGGIE WHITE (1961–2004)
DEFENSIVE END
PHILADELPHIA EAGLES SEASONS: 1985–92; GREEN BAY PACKERS SEASONS: 1993–98; CAROLINA PANTHERS SEASON: 2000
HALL OF FAME CLASS: 2006
AWARDS/HONORS: MEMBER OF NFL 75TH/100TH ANNIVERSARY TEAMS, 13X PRO BOWL, 13X ALL-PRO (8X FIRST TEAM), 1980S/1990S NFL ALL-DECADE TEAMS, 2X NFL DEFENSIVE PLAYER OF THE YEAR, NFL DEFENSIVE ROOKIE OF THE YEAR, SUPER BOWL CHAMPION

Reggie White was nicknamed the "Minister of Defense" because he was a real ordained minister. He started his pro football career in 1984 with the Memphis Showboats of the U.S. Football League. When the league folded in 1985, White joined the NFL's Philadelphia Eagles. He recorded 13 sacks his first year and was named NFL Defensive Rookie of the Year. That started a string of nine straight double-digit sack seasons—an NFL record. He recorded NFL-leading totals of 21 sacks in 1987 (in just 12 games) and 18 sacks in 1988. White earned the first of two NFL Defensive Player of the Year awards in 1987.

White became a free agent following the 1992 season. He signed with the Green Bay Packers. A few years later, with his help, Green Bay won its first Super Bowl in nearly 30 years. White set a Super Bowl record with three sacks in Super Bowl XXXI (31). Two seasons later, he earned his second NFL Defensive Player of the Year award.

White retired in 2000 as the NFL's all-time sack leader with 198. Counting his two years with Memphis, White collected 221.5 career sacks. He was named All-Pro 13 of his 15 NFL seasons. That included eight First Team nods. He also played in 13 Pro Bowls. "My goal as a football player was to be the best to ever play my position," he said. "I believe I've reached my goal."

BRUCE SMITH

BRUCE SMITH (1963–)
DEFENSIVE END
BUFFALO BILLS SEASONS: 1985–99; WASHINGTON REDSKINS SEASONS: 2000–03
HALL OF FAME CLASS: 2009
AWARDS/HONORS: MEMBER OF 100TH ANNIVERSARY TEAM, 11X PRO BOWL, 11X ALL-PRO (9X FIRST TEAM), 1980S/1990S NFL ALL-DECADE TEAMS, 2X NFL DEFENSIVE PLAYER OF THE YEAR

The Buffalo Bills selected Bruce Smith with the first overall choice of the 1985 NFL Draft out of Virginia Tech. It was one of the greatest first overall draft choices of all time. Smith recorded an NFL record with 200 career sacks. Twice, he was named NFL Defensive Player of the Year (DPOY). He earned 9 First Team All-Pro selections and played in 11 Pro Bowls. In 12 of his 14 seasons playing in Buffalo, Smith had double-digit sack totals. He sacked a career-high 19 quarterbacks in 1990.

The Bills were not a good team when Smith arrived. They won just two games that season. But by 1988, they had won a division title for the first time since 1980. And by 1990, the Bills were in their first Super Bowl. Smith was a key reason for the success. He recorded the first of his DPOY honors in 1990. The Bills were a last-second field goal away from becoming Super Bowl champions that season. That year was the first of Buffalo's four straight Super Bowl appearances. The team was not able to win the big one though.

Smith was named DPOY again in 1996, with 13.5 sacks for the season. He played the last four seasons of his career with Washington. He was the only player in NFL history to record at least one sack in each of 19 seasons. And he was the only player to record at least 10 sacks in each of 13 seasons.

93
NIKE
NIKE

JOHN RANDLE

JOHN RANDLE (1967–)
DEFENSIVE TACKLE
MINNESOTA VIKINGS SEASONS: 1990–2000; SEATTLE SEAHAWKS SEASONS: 2001–03
HALL OF FAME CLASS: 2010
AWARDS/HONORS: MEMBER OF 100TH ANNIVERSARY TEAM, 7X PRO BOWL, 6X FIRST TEAM ALL-PRO, 1990S NFL ALL-DECADE TEAM

One of the unlikeliest members of the Pro Football Hall of Fame is John Randle. He started his career at a community college before transferring to Texas A&I (now Texas A&M University-Kingsville). Considered too small to play defensive tackle, Randle went undrafted. He tried out for the Tampa Bay Buccaneers, but they didn't sign him. He finally caught on with the Minnesota Vikings. In his 1990 rookie season, he played in all 16 games. Randle became a full-time starter in 1992 and recorded the first of nine double-digit sack seasons with 11.5. In 1993, he earned the first of six straight First Team All-Pro and Pro Bowl appearances after posting 12.5 sacks. He led the NFL in 1997 with 15.5 sacks.

Randle's favorite quarterback to sack may have been Brett Favre. Favre played for the rival Green Bay Packers. Favre said Randle was the toughest defensive player he had ever faced. Randle recorded a career-high 3.5 sacks on Favre and the Packers in a 1996 game. He collected 137.5 sacks over his 14-year career. That's the most ever by a defensive tackle. Randle made his final Pro Bowl appearance with the Seattle Seahawks in 2001.

Randle loved playing football. He was well known for painting his face before every game. He trash-talked on the field, too. "This is like being a kid, having fun and being animated," he said. "If I didn't do any of this, I would be too mechanical, too uptight."

WARREN SAPP

WARREN SAPP (1972–)
DEFENSIVE TACKLE
TAMPA BAY BUCCANEERS SEASONS: 1995–2003; OAKLAND RAIDERS SEASONS: 2004–07
HALL OF FAME CLASS: 2013
AWARDS/HONORS: 7X PRO BOWL, 6X ALL-PRO (4X FIRST TEAM), 1990S/2000S NFL ALL-DECADE TEAMS, NFL DEFENSIVE PLAYER OF THE YEAR, SUPER BOWL CHAMPION

From 1983 to 1994, the Tampa Bay Buccaneers were the worst team in the NFL. Their record was 51–140. They lost at least 10 games every season. But their fortune changed in 1995. In the first round of the NFL Draft, they selected defensive tackle Warren Sapp with the 12th overall pick. They then selected linebacker Derrick Brooks. Sapp would stay with the team 9 years, Brooks 14. Both would later be elected to the Pro Football Hall of Fame.

Sapp led the team's defensive turnaround. By 1997, Sapp's third season, Tampa Bay was in the playoffs for the first time in 15 seasons. Sapp earned his first Pro Bowl nod that season. Two years later, he was named NFL Defensive Player of the Year. He had collected 12.5 sacks and led Tampa Bay to the NFC Championship Game.

Sapp and the Tampa Bay defense continued to rule. Sapp had a career-high 16.5 sacks in 2000. In 2002, he earned his fourth straight First Team All-Pro honor. The Buccaneers made their first Super Bowl appearance, too. Sapp was part of the charge that resulted in three defensive touchdowns. The Bucs routed the Oakland Raiders for their first Super Bowl title.

Sapp finished his career with Oakland. He recorded 10 sacks in 2006. For his career, he collected 96.5 sacks, third most for a defensive tackle.

POSITION CHANGES

While still considered the biggest players on defense, defensive linemen are becoming quicker and more agile. Defensive ends are sometimes referred to as "edge rushers." They are a mixture of a defensive end and a linebacker. They mainly rush the quarterback and stop the run. But they can also drop back into pass coverage. T. J. Watt of the Pittsburgh Steelers is a good example of an edge rusher. There are still some giant defensive tackles, but they are now expected to be quicker, stronger athletes who can do more than just fill the gaps.

83
BROWNS
83
ny
Wilson

MICHAEL STRAHAN

MICHAEL STRAHAN (1971–)
DEFENSIVE END
NEW YORK GIANTS SEASONS: 1993–2007
HALL OF FAME CLASS: 2014
AWARDS/HONORS: 7X PRO BOWL, 6X ALL-PRO (4X FIRST TEAM), 2000S NFL ALL-DECADE TEAM, NFL DEFENSIVE PLAYER OF THE YEAR, SUPER BOWL CHAMPION

One Hall of Famer who may have become more recognizable *after* his playing career is Michael Strahan. He's everywhere today: on television news programs, NFL pre-game shows, and game shows. Before his TV career, however, he was a powerhouse in opposing teams' backfields.

Strahan was taken in the second round of the 1993 NFL Draft by the New York Giants. He played his entire 15-year career with them. Twice, he led the Giants to the Super Bowl. In the final game of his career, Strahan had two tackles and one sack. The Giants beat the undefeated New England Patriots in Super Bowl XLII (42). It was one of the biggest upsets in sports history.

One sack is all Strahan recorded in his rookie season. He achieved his first double-digit sack season in 1997 with 14. He earned his first Pro Bowl nod and First Team All-Pro selection that season. He had one of the greatest seasons of all time in 2001. During it, he set an NFL record with 22.5 sacks. He also led the league with 24 tackles for loss and 7 forced fumbles. He was named NFL Defensive Player of the Year. Two years later, Strahan led the league again in sacks with 18.5.

Nothing can hold Strahan down, not even gravity! In 2021, he went to outer space aboard the Blue Origin spaceflight mission. At 6-feet-5-inches tall, he became the tallest person ever to fly in space.

INDEX

Brooks, Derrick, 28
Buffalo Bills, 24
changes in position, 29
Dallas Cowboys, 13, 19, 21
defensive linemen duties, 8, 11
Denver Broncos, 19
Favre, Brett, 27
"Fearsome Foursome," 10
Green Bay Packers, 23, 27
Greene, "Mean" Joe, 14
Jones, David "Deacon," 10, 20
Lilly, Bob "Mr. Cowboy," 13
Los Angeles Rams, 10, 20, 21
Martin, Harvey, 19
Miami Dolphins, 13
Minnesota Vikings, 16, 27
New England Patriots, 31
New York Giants, 31
NFL Defensive Player of the Year, 10, 13, 14, 16, 19, 23, 24, 28, 31
NFL Defensive Rookie of the Year, 14, 23
NFL Draft, 13, 14, 19, 20, 24, 28, 31
NFL Man of the Year, 14
NFL Most Valuable Player, 16
Oakland Raiders, 28
Olsen, Merlin, 10
Page, Alan, 16
Philadelphia Eagles, 23
Pittsburgh Steelers, 14, 21, 29
"Purple People Eaters" defense, 16
Randle, John, 27
sacks, 8, 10, 13, 16, 19, 20, 23, 24, 27, 28, 31
San Diego Chargers, 10
Sapp, Warren, 28
Seattle Seahawks, 27
Smith, Bruce, 24
St. Louis Cardinals, 20
"Steel Curtain" defense, 14
Strahan, Michael, 31
Super Bowl, 13, 14, 16, 19, 20, 21, 23, 24, 28, 31
Tampa Bay Buccaneers, 21, 27, 28
Washington Redskins, 24
Watt, T. J., 29
White, Randy "the Manster," 19
White, Reggie "Minister of Defense," 8, 23
Youngblood, Jack, 20, 21